2019 SUCCESS JOURNAL

"The future belongs to those who believe in the beauty of their dreams"

- Eleanor Roosevelt

This year belongs to

_____

Written by: Mackenzie Reed

Created by: Journal Mastery

The Magic of this Journal

Have you tried making exciting New Year's resolutions previous years and then not had exciting results?

Of course you have, we all have, but now you have taken the first step to drastically changing the outcome of your resolutions.

An effective way to reach your goals is to first identify them and write them down. However, to make 2019 extraordinary, it is not enough to write down your New Year's resolutions once in the beginning of the year.

To ensure your success, it will require continuous planning, tracking, and a ton of motivation in the process during the whole year. Choosing the right goals also requires efficient journal prompts designed just for that.

When you set an intention and continuously focus on it, eventually it will come true.

The Truth About Journaling for Success

Working on your goals with effective action steps is the most important part of the success quest.

Planning and tracking are actually just a helpful tool and should not be the work that takes up most of the time. In fact, it should take the least time possible while being as effective as possible.

The power of the *2019 Success Journal* is that it's kept simple with the most powerful exercises. It is not at all required that you spend 15-30 minutes per day for a whole year. It is not necessary, and pretty much nobody will ever succeed doing that. The motivation would die quickly.

In the *2019 Success Journal,* you can write just once a week for about 10 minutes, and then you will be on track with your goals all year long.

You can throughout the year browse through your journal when you need to and get the motivation and inspiration that it provides without having to do anymore work in the success journal.

Do you want to make 2019 your best year ever?

Chances are that it will not happen without some effort on your side. Actually, you might not even want to reach your successes effortlessly. Reaching your goals through exerting focused effort while tracking your results feels amazing, and you will most likely cherish and celebrate your success much more this way.

How to Use the Journal

To get the most out of your journal, follow these simple guidelines.

Beginning of the year

1. Write down your success goals for the whole year on the pages "My 2019 Success Goals." The pages are left blank, so you can write all your goals and also add whatever else you like such as drawings and photos if you feel like it.

   Pictures can help as a visual booster and complement the written goals. On the following pages, you can write down additional visions for 2019. Fill out the ones that inspire you and leave the rest.

2. Afterwards you are asked to write down your sub goals for the first 3 to 6 months, so you know what you want to accomplish in a shorter time frame. These can be goals that are accomplished during the year like running a marathon. Some yearlong goals will have consecutive time frames such as reaching a certain amount of sales, and then it can be helpful to have some sub goals along the way.

Beginning of each month

1. You are asked to fill out an initial rating (1-10) on the different areas of life every month. In this way, you can keep track of your monthly progress.

2. From February forward, you will have the opportunity to review the past month and list any loose ends.

3. On the following pages write down what you will like to accomplish that month.

4. Finally, you can create your "daily routine" overview that you can use to stay on track daily. Your daily routines are to a large extent what will make or break achieving your goals, so this is an important part of your planning.

Once every week

Every week of the month has a "beginning of the week" exercise and an "end of the week" exercise.
You can do all the weekly exercises once a week, e.g., every Sunday, where you track the week that has gone and plan for the next. In that way, you can make it a habit to set aside a little time for the journal and success quest every Sunday.

End of the month

In the end, you can reflect on the month's highlights and give an overall rating of the whole month.

Repetition

You will throughout the year be asked to repeat the goals you have set for yourself. This is a powerful way of reminding your mind what you want. The more you focus on your goals, the better it is. For this reason, I strongly encourage you to revisit your 2019 Success Goals as often as you open the book. When you browse through the pages, try to get in touch with the feelings of excitement and belief that you felt when you created the pages.

More journaling?

If you want to journal on a daily basis, you can use an additional journal for that. It is very important that you feel motivated for your journal writing and don't make it another mundane task or duty. Keeping it simple yet exciting is key.

Hopefully, you will feel excited to track your weekly and monthly success and progress with this journal.

Keep a Positive Focus

As you will probably notice, in many of the exercises you get the chance to reflect on and track your *successes* and what's *working* more than what's not working. This is a way for you to keep motivation and is a direct result of implementing the law of attraction: What you focus on is what you get. I encourage you to reflect a bit on your challenges and track any missing results, but it should not be your main focus. I find this to be a powerful way to reach your goals while enjoying the process as well as increasing your own self-esteem.

Writing is a powerful tool, and I believe you shouldn't have to write down everything you haven't done or that didn't work. You already know that in your head, and you can implement those things in the planning for the next week or month.

Choosing Your 2019 Goals

Choosing your goals for 2019 is not necessarily easy. Maybe you know which direction you want to go but are not 100% sure exactly what you really want.

Your goals for 2019 can be related to different areas of life, and most likely you want to make progress in all areas, but some things might be more important than others. Acknowledge that and work primarily towards the things that are most important for you to accomplish.

When deciding your goals, one thing to keep in mind is that there is a difference between short-term realistic goals and long-term unrealistic goals also called visions. You might find that a combination of both is the best way to decide your goals. What makes a goal short-term or long-term is not an exact science. It very much depends on your own point of view of what is realistic and unrealistic.

> You may get to the very top of the ladder only to find out that it was all along placed against the wrong wall.

As a rule of thumb, short-term goals are probably achievable within a year. However, a long-term unrealistic goal can also become realistic and achieved within a year with the right focus, planning, tracking, help, and motivation.

When planning for your one-year goals, it can be beneficial to look a bit further ahead for the right direction. Long-term goals can help with that.

I find that creating an actual life vision can be a bit overwhelming and actually set a stop for the magic of the unknown, so I don't recommend doing that. Having a long-term vision (1-3 years) and knowing yourself and your values is the best way to create the right direction for you.

Short-term goals

An effective way to work with short-term goals is to specify them with the so-called S.M.A.R.T. goals model. It is a famous model coaching tool for goal setting and in my opinion very helpful for your short-term goal-setting (within one year).

The S.M.A.R.T. model:

- Specific
- Measurable
- Achievable
- Realistic
- Time limited

Make sure your short-term goals comply with all 5 requirements. There are many resources online that cover the S.M.A.R.T model in more depth, should you want to dive a bit deeper.

Long-term goals – visions

When deciding on a long-term goal, you can apply this very simple technique that has proven to be the best chance of reaching goals. Creating your vision this way, there is a better chance that you will feel you are on the right track of life and living with an appealing purpose. To reach your vision, there should be an equal amount of **excitement** and **belief** that you can actually achieve it. If one of them fails, the vision might not be right for you, and you will likely unintentionally set yourself up for failure.

For your long-term goals to be exciting enough for you to persevere and finally reach them, any goal should be a minimum of 7 on an excitement scale from 1-10.

Likewise, to be successful, the goal should be a minimum of 7 on a belief scale from 1-10.

Which goals meet both criteria for you?

Final Recommendations

Remember, a journal is meant to be used, and you can't make any mistakes! If you write something you didn't really mean, then congratulate yourself for realizing that and for getting to know yourself even better.

The *2019 Success Journal* is just a journal filled with pieces of paper. You can do whatever you want with it. If you only use it a bit, then that's better than nothing. You can pick and choose exercises as you wish.

Your success however depends on the amount of effective effort you put into it. That goes for your daily action steps as well as working with this journal. All the exercises are designed for making progress. You can hardly avoid making any kind of progress no matter how few of the exercises you do, as long as you are consistent throughout the year.

If you have a hard time getting started, a good trick is to start writing any immediate thoughts on a separate blank piece of paper. The best writing and your deeper thoughts and feelings often come out after a short period of warm-up writing.

To your success!

Mackenzie Reed

PLANNING THE YEAR

My 2019 Success Goals

I want to travel here in 2019

I want to read these books in 2019

I would like for this to happen in 2019

I want to develop these skills in 2019

My 6-Month Goals

By June 30, 2019, I have accomplished:

My 3-Month Goals

By March 31, 2019, I have accomplished:

_____

_____

_____

_____

_____

_____

_____

_____

_____

_____

_____

_____

JANUARY

Relationships	1	2	3	4	5	6	7	8	9	10
Health	1	2	3	4	5	6	7	8	9	10
Finances	1	2	3	4	5	6	7	8	9	10
Productivity	1	2	3	4	5	6	7	8	9	10
Creativity	1	2	3	4	5	6	7	8	9	10
Job/business	1	2	3	4	5	6	7	8	9	10
Self-esteem	1	2	3	4	5	6	7	8	9	10
Happiness	1	2	3	4	5	6	7	8	9	10

I want to experience these exciting, fun, joyful things in January

I want to read these books in January

_____

_____

_____

_____

_____

By January 31, I'm better at

_____

_____

_____

_____

_____

My Daily Routine

Morning

Day

Evening

My 3-Month Goals

By March 31, 2019:

_____

_____

_____

_____

_____

_____

My January Goals

By January 31, 2019:

_____

_____

_____

_____

_____

_____

Week

Beginning of the week

"The secret of getting ahead is getting started"

– Mark Twain

In order to reach my goals, I will this week

_____

_____

_____

_____

_____

_____

_____

This week will be great because

_____

_____

_____

_____

End of the week

Did I practice gratitude this week ?

My personal successes this week

_____

_____

_____

_____

_____

_____

_____

Highlights of the week

_____

_____

_____

_____

_____

_____

Week success	1 2 3 4 5 6 7 8 9 10
Felt alive this week	1 2 3 4 5 6 7 8 9 10
Daily routine success	1 2 3 4 5 6 7 8 9 10

Week

Beginning of the week
Did I reach previous week's goals?

My January goals

_____

_____

_____

_____

_____

In order to reach my goals, I will this week

_____

_____

_____

_____

_____

This week will be great because

_____

_____

_____

_____

End of the week
Did I practice gratitude this week?

My personal successes this week

_____

_____

_____

_____

_____

_____

_____

Highlights of the week

_____

_____

_____

_____

_____

_____

_____

Week success	1 2 3 4 5 6 7 8 9 10
Felt alive this week	1 2 3 4 5 6 7 8 9 10
Daily routine success	1 2 3 4 5 6 7 8 9 10

Week

My January goals

_____

_____

_____

_____

_____

_____

_____

In order to reach my goals, I will this week

_____

_____

_____

_____

_____

_____

This week will be great because

_____

_____

_____

_____

End of the week

Did I express love this week?

My personal successes this week

_____

_____

_____

_____

_____

_____

_____

Highlights of the week

_____

_____

_____

_____

_____

_____

Week success	1	2	3	4	5	6	7	8	9	10
Felt alive this week	1	2	3	4	5	6	7	8	9	10
Daily routine success	1	2	3	4	5	6	7	8	9	10

Week

Beginning of the week
Did I reach previous week's goals?

My January goals

_____

_____

_____

_____

_____

_____

In order to reach my goals, I will this week

_____

_____

_____

_____

_____

_____

This week will be great because

_____

_____

_____

_____

End of the week
Did I drink enough water this week?

My personal successes this week

_____

_____

_____

_____

_____

_____

Highlights of the week

_____

_____

_____

_____

_____

_____

Week success	1 2 3 4 5 6 7 8 9 10
Felt alive this week	1 2 3 4 5 6 7 8 9 10
Daily routine success	1 2 3 4 5 6 7 8 9 10

January Highlights

Month Overall Success   1   2   3   4   5   6   7   8   9   10

FEBRUARY

Relationships	1	2	3	4	5	6	7	8	9	10
Health	1	2	3	4	5	6	7	8	9	10
Finances	1	2	3	4	5	6	7	8	9	10
Productivity	1	2	3	4	5	6	7	8	9	10
Creativity	1	2	3	4	5	6	7	8	9	10
Job/business	1	2	3	4	5	6	7	8	9	10
Self-esteem	1	2	3	4	5	6	7	8	9	10
Happiness	1	2	3	4	5	6	7	8	9	10

Last month review and loose ends

I want to experience these exciting, fun, joyful things in February

I want to read these books in February

By February 28, I'm better at

My Daily Routine

Morning

Day

Evening

My 3-month Goals

By March 31, 2019 I have

_____

_____

_____

_____

_____

My February Goals

By February 28, 2019 I have

_____

_____

_____

_____

_____

Week

Beginning of the week

"Do one thing every day that scares you"

— Eleanor Roosevelt

In order to reach my goals, I will this week

_____

_____

_____

_____

_____

_____

This week will be great because

_____

_____

_____

_____

End of the week

Did I practice gratitude this week?

My personal successes this week

_____

_____

_____

_____

_____

_____

Highlights of the week

_____

_____

_____

_____

_____

_____

Week success	1	2	3	4	5	6	7	8	9	10
Felt alive this week	1	2	3	4	5	6	7	8	9	10
Daily routine success	1	2	3	4	5	6	7	8	9	10

Week

Beginning of the week
Did I reach previous week's goals?

My February goals

_____

_____

_____

_____

_____

In order to reach my goals, I will this week

_____

_____

_____

_____

_____

This week will be great because

_____

_____

_____

_____

End of the week
Did I have fun this week?

My personal successes this week

Highlights of the week

Week success	1	2	3	4	5	6	7	8	9	10
Felt alive this week	1	2	3	4	5	6	7	8	9	10
Daily routine success	1	2	3	4	5	6	7	8	9	10

Week

Beginning of the week
Did I reach previous week's goals?

My February goals

_____

_____

_____

_____

_____

In order to reach my goals, I will this week

_____

_____

_____

_____

_____

This week will be great because

_____

_____

_____

_____

End of the week

Did I work on my creativity this week?

My personal successes this week

_____

_____

_____

_____

_____

_____

Highlights of the week

_____

_____

_____

_____

_____

_____

Week success	1 2 3 4 5 6 7 8 9 10
Felt alive this week	1 2 3 4 5 6 7 8 9 10
Daily routine success	1 2 3 4 5 6 7 8 9 10

Week

Beginning of the week
Did I reach previous week's goals?

My February goals

_____

_____

_____

_____

_____

_____

In order to reach my goals, I will this week

_____

_____

_____

_____

_____

_____

This week will be great because

_____

_____

_____

_____

End of the week

Did I practice gratitude this week?

My personal successes this week

_____
_____
_____
_____
_____
_____

Highlights of the week

_____
_____
_____
_____
_____
_____

Week success	1 2 3 4 5 6 7 8 9 10
Felt alive this week	1 2 3 4 5 6 7 8 9 10
Daily routine success	1 2 3 4 5 6 7 8 9 10

Week

Beginning of the week
Did I reach previous week's goals?

My February goals

_____

_____

_____

_____

_____

_____

In order to reach my goals, I will this week

_____

_____

_____

_____

_____

_____

This week will be great because

_____

_____

_____

_____

End of the week

Did I drink enough water this week?

My personal successes this week

_____

_____

_____

_____

_____

_____

Highlights of the week

_____

_____

_____

_____

_____

_____

Week success	1 2 3 4 5 6 7 8 9 10
Felt alive this week	1 2 3 4 5 6 7 8 9 10
Daily routine success	1 2 3 4 5 6 7 8 9 10

February Highlights

Month Overall Success   1   2   3   4   5   6   7   8   9   10

MARCH

Relationships	1	2	3	4	5	6	7	8	9	10
Health	1	2	3	4	5	6	7	8	9	10
Finances	1	2	3	4	5	6	7	8	9	10
Productivity	1	2	3	4	5	6	7	8	9	10
Creativity	1	2	3	4	5	6	7	8	9	10
Job/business	1	2	3	4	5	6	7	8	9	10
Self-esteem	1	2	3	4	5	6	7	8	9	10
Happiness	1	2	3	4	5	6	7	8	9	10

Last month review and loose ends

I want to experience these exciting, fun, joyful things in March

I want to read these books in March

_____

_____

_____

_____

_____

By March 31, I'm better at

_____

_____

_____

_____

_____

My Daily Routine

Morning

Day

Evening

My 3 Month Goals

By March 31, 2019 I have

_____

_____

_____

_____

_____

_____

My March Goals

By March 31, 2019 I have (if different from above)

_____

_____

_____

_____

_____

Week

"If you are going through hell, keep going"

— Winston Churchill

In order to reach my goals, I will this week

_____

_____

_____

_____

_____

_____

This week will be great because

_____

_____

_____

_____

End of the week

Did I have fun this week?

My personal successes this week

_____

_____

_____

_____

_____

_____

Highlights of the week

_____

_____

_____

_____

_____

_____

Week success	1	2	3	4	5	6	7	8	9	10
Felt alive this week	1	2	3	4	5	6	7	8	9	10
Daily routine success	1	2	3	4	5	6	7	8	9	10

Week

My March goals

_____

_____

_____

_____

_____

_____

In order to reach my goals, I will this week

_____

_____

_____

_____

_____

This week will be great because

_____

_____

_____

_____

End of the week

Did I drink enough water this week?

My personal successes this week

_____

_____

_____

_____

_____

_____

Highlights of the week

_____

_____

_____

_____

_____

_____

Week success	1 2 3 4 5 6 7 8 9 10
Felt alive this week	1 2 3 4 5 6 7 8 9 10
Daily routine success	1 2 3 4 5 6 7 8 9 10

Week

Beginning of the week
Did I reach previous week's goals?

My March goals

In order to reach my goals, I will this week

This week will be great because

End of the week

Did I practice gratitude this week?

My personal successes this week

_____

_____

_____

_____

_____

_____

Highlights of the week

_____

_____

_____

_____

_____

_____

Week success		1 2 3 4 5 6 7 8 9 10
Felt alive this week		1 2 3 4 5 6 7 8 9 10
Daily routine success		1 2 3 4 5 6 7 8 9 10

Week

My March goals

_____

_____

_____

_____

_____

_____

In order to reach my goals, I will this week

_____

_____

_____

_____

_____

_____

This week will be great because

_____

_____

_____

_____

End of the week

Did I express love this week?

My personal successes this week

_____

_____

_____

_____

_____

_____

_____

Highlights of the week

_____

_____

_____

_____

_____

_____

_____

Week success	1 2 3 4 5 6 7 8 9 10
Felt alive this week	1 2 3 4 5 6 7 8 9 10
Daily routine success	1 2 3 4 5 6 7 8 9 10

Week

Beginning of the week
Did I reach previous week's goals?

My March goals

_____

_____

_____

_____

_____

_____

In order to reach my goals, I will this week

_____

_____

_____

_____

_____

_____

This week will be great because

_____

_____

_____

_____

End of the week

Did I practice gratitude this week ?

My personal successes this week

_____

_____

_____

_____

_____

_____

Highlights of the week

_____

_____

_____

_____

_____

_____

Week success	1	2	3	4	5	6	7	8	9	10
Felt alive this week	1	2	3	4	5	6	7	8	9	10
Daily routine success	1	2	3	4	5	6	7	8	9	10

Week

Beginning of the week
Did I reach previous week's goals?

My March goals

_____

_____

_____

_____

_____

_____

In order to reach my goals, I will this week

_____

_____

_____

_____

_____

_____

This week will be great because

_____

_____

_____

_____

End of the week

Did I drink enough water this week?

My personal successes this week

_____

_____

_____

_____

_____

_____

_____

Highlights of the week

_____

_____

_____

_____

_____

_____

Week success   1 2 3 4 5 6 7 8 9 10
Felt alive this week   1 2 3 4 5 6 7 8 9 10
Daily routine success   1 2 3 4 5 6 7 8 9 10

March Highlights

Month Overall Success   1   2   3   4   5   6   7   8   9   10

APRIL

Relationships	1	2	3	4	5	6	7	8	9	10
Health	1	2	3	4	5	6	7	8	9	10
Finances	1	2	3	4	5	6	7	8	9	10
Productivity	1	2	3	4	5	6	7	8	9	10
Creativity	1	2	3	4	5	6	7	8	9	10
Job/business	1	2	3	4	5	6	7	8	9	10
Self-esteem	1	2	3	4	5	6	7	8	9	10
Happiness	1	2	3	4	5	6	7	8	9	10

Last month review and loose ends

I want to experience these exciting, fun, joyful things in April

I want to read these books in April

_____

_____

_____

_____

_____

By 30th of April I'm better at

_____

_____

_____

_____

My Daily Routine

Morning

Day

Evening

My 3-Month Goals

By June 30, 2019 I have

_____

_____

_____

_____

_____

My April Goals

By April 30, 2019 I have

_____

_____

_____

_____

_____

Week

Beginning of the week

"Happiness lies in the joy of achievement and the thrill of creative effort"

– Mark Twain

In order to reach my goals, I will this week

_____

_____

_____

_____

_____

_____

_____

This week will be great because

_____

_____

_____

_____

End of the week
Did I have fun this week?

My personal successes this week

_____

_____

_____

_____

_____

_____

_____

Highlights of the week

_____

_____

_____

_____

_____

_____

_____

Week success	1 2 3 4 5 6 7 8 9 10
Felt alive this week	1 2 3 4 5 6 7 8 9 10
Daily routine success	1 2 3 4 5 6 7 8 9 10

Week

Beginning of the week
Did I reach previous week's goals?

My April goals

In order to reach my goals, I will this week

This week will be great because

End of the week
Did I drink enough water this week?

My personal successes this week

_____

_____

_____

_____

_____

_____

Highlights of the week

_____

_____

_____

_____

_____

_____

Week success	1 2 3 4 5 6 7 8 9 10
Felt alive this week	1 2 3 4 5 6 7 8 9 10
Daily routine success	1 2 3 4 5 6 7 8 9 10

Week

Beginning of the week
Did I reach previous week's goals?

My April goals

_____

_____

_____

_____

_____

_____

In order to reach my goals, I will this week

_____

_____

_____

_____

_____

_____

This week will be great because

_____

_____

_____

_____

End of the week

Did I express love this week?

My personal successes this week

_____

_____

_____

_____

_____

_____

_____

Highlights of the week

_____

_____

_____

_____

_____

_____

Week success	1 2 3 4 5 6 7 8 9 10
Felt alive this week	1 2 3 4 5 6 7 8 9 10
Daily routine success	1 2 3 4 5 6 7 8 9 10

Week

Beginning of the week
Did I reach previous week's goals?

My April goals

_____

_____

_____

_____

_____

_____

In order to reach my goals, I will this week

_____

_____

_____

_____

_____

_____

This week will be great because

_____

_____

_____

_____

End of the week

Did I contribute to others this week?

My personal successes this week

_____

_____

_____

_____

_____

_____

Highlights of the week

_____

_____

_____

_____

_____

_____

Week success	1	2	3	4	5	6	7	8	9	10
Felt alive this week	1	2	3	4	5	6	7	8	9	10
Daily routine success	1	2	3	4	5	6	7	8	9	10

Week

My April goals

_____

_____

_____

_____

_____

_____

In order to reach my goals, I will this week

_____

_____

_____

_____

_____

_____

This week will be great because

_____

_____

_____

_____

End of the week

Did I practice gratitude this week?

My personal successes this week

_____

_____

_____

_____

_____

_____

Highlights of the week

_____

_____

_____

_____

_____

_____

Week success	1	2	3	4	5	6	7	8	9	10
Felt alive this week	1	2	3	4	5	6	7	8	9	10
Daily routine success	1	2	3	4	5	6	7	8	9	10

April Highlights

Month Overall Success   1   2   3   4   5   6   7   8   9   10

MAY

Relationships	1	2	3	4	5	6	7	8	9	10
Health	1	2	3	4	5	6	7	8	9	10
Finances	1	2	3	4	5	6	7	8	9	10
Productivity	1	2	3	4	5	6	7	8	9	10
Creativity	1	2	3	4	5	6	7	8	9	10
Job/business	1	2	3	4	5	6	7	8	9	10
Self-esteem	1	2	3	4	5	6	7	8	9	10
Happiness	1	2	3	4	5	6	7	8	9	10

Last month review and loose ends

I want to experience these exciting, fun, joyful things in May

I want to read these books in May

_____

_____

_____

_____

_____

By May 31, I'm better at

_____

_____

_____

_____

My Daily Routine

Morning

Day

Evening

My 3-Month Goals

By June 30, 2019 I have

_____

_____

_____

_____

_____

_____

My May Goals

By May 31, 2019 I have

_____

_____

_____

_____

_____

_____

Week

"Don't be afraid to give up something good to go for the great"

— John D. Rockefeller

In order to reach my goals, I will this week

_____

_____

_____

_____

_____

_____

This week will be great because

_____

_____

_____

_____

End of the week
Did I have fun this week?

My personal successes this week

_____

_____

_____

_____

_____

_____

_____

Highlights of the week

_____

_____

_____

_____

_____

_____

_____

Week success	1	2	3	4	5	6	7	8	9	10
Felt alive this week	1	2	3	4	5	6	7	8	9	10
Daily routine success	1	2	3	4	5	6	7	8	9	10

Week

Beginning of the week
Did I reach previous week's goals?

My May goals

_____

_____

_____

_____

_____

_____

In order to reach my goals, I will this week

_____

_____

_____

_____

_____

_____

This week will be great because

_____

_____

_____

_____

End of the week

Did I practice gratitude this week ?

My personal successes this week

_____

_____

_____

_____

_____

_____

Highlights of the week

_____

_____

_____

_____

_____

_____

Week success	1 2 3 4 5 6 7 8 9 10
Felt alive this week	1 2 3 4 5 6 7 8 9 10
Daily routine success	1 2 3 4 5 6 7 8 9 10

Week

My May goals

_____

_____

_____

_____

_____

_____

In order to reach my goals, I will this week

_____

_____

_____

_____

_____

_____

This week will be great because

_____

_____

_____

_____

End of the week
Did I enjoy life this week?

My personal successes this week

_____

_____

_____

_____

_____

_____

Highlights of the week

_____

_____

_____

_____

_____

_____

Week success	1	2	3	4	5	6	7	8	9	10
Felt alive this week	1	2	3	4	5	6	7	8	9	10
Daily routine success	1	2	3	4	5	6	7	8	9	10

Week

My May goals

_____

_____

_____

_____

_____

_____

In order to reach my goals, I will this week

_____

_____

_____

_____

_____

_____

This week will be great because

_____

_____

_____

_____

End of the week
Did I express love this week?

My personal successes this week

_____

_____

_____

_____

_____

_____

Highlights of the week

_____

_____

_____

_____

_____

_____

Week success	1 2 3 4 5 6 7 8 9 10
Felt alive this week	1 2 3 4 5 6 7 8 9 10
Daily routine success	1 2 3 4 5 6 7 8 9 10

Week

Beginning of the week
Did I reach previous week's goals?

My May goals

_____
_____
_____
_____
_____
_____

In order to reach my goals, I will this week

_____
_____
_____
_____
_____
_____

This week will be great because

_____
_____
_____
_____

End of the week

Did I drink enough water this week?

My personal successes this week

_____

_____

_____

_____

_____

_____

_____

Highlights of the week

_____

_____

_____

_____

_____

_____

_____

Week success	1	2	3	4	5	6	7	8	9	10
Felt alive this week	1	2	3	4	5	6	7	8	9	10
Daily routine success	1	2	3	4	5	6	7	8	9	10

May Highlights

Month Overall Success   1   2   3   4   5   6   7   8   9   10

JUNE

Relationships	1	2	3	4	5	6	7	8	9	10
Health	1	2	3	4	5	6	7	8	9	10
Finances	1	2	3	4	5	6	7	8	9	10
Productivity	1	2	3	4	5	6	7	8	9	10
Creativity	1	2	3	4	5	6	7	8	9	10
Job/business	1	2	3	4	5	6	7	8	9	10
Self-esteem	1	2	3	4	5	6	7	8	9	10
Happiness	1	2	3	4	5	6	7	8	9	10

Last month review and loose ends

I want to experience these exciting, fun, joyful things in June

I want to read these books in June

_____

_____

_____

_____

_____

By 30th of June I'm better at

_____

_____

_____

_____

_____

My Daily Routine

Morning

Day

Evening

My 3-Month Goals

By June 30, 2019 I have

_____

_____

_____

_____

_____

_____

My June Goals

By June 30, 2019 I have (if different from above)

_____

_____

_____

_____

_____

_____

Week

Beginning of the week

"I find that the more I work, the more luck I seem to have"

– Thomas Jefferson

In order to reach my goals, I will this week

_____

_____

_____

_____

_____

_____

This week will be great because

_____

_____

_____

_____

End of the week
Did I have fun this week?

My personal successes this week

_____

_____

_____

_____

_____

_____

Highlights of the week

_____

_____

_____

_____

_____

_____

Week success	1	2	3	4	5	6	7	8	9	10
Felt alive this week	1	2	3	4	5	6	7	8	9	10
Daily routine success	1	2	3	4	5	6	7	8	9	10

Week

My June goals

_____

_____

_____

_____

_____

_____

In order to reach my goals, I will this week

_____

_____

_____

_____

_____

_____

This week will be great because

_____

_____

_____

_____

End of the week
Did I drink enough water this week?

My personal successes this week

_____

_____

_____

_____

_____

_____

Highlights of the week

_____

_____

_____

_____

_____

_____

Week success	1 2 3 4 5 6 7 8 9 10
Felt alive this week	1 2 3 4 5 6 7 8 9 10
Daily routine success	1 2 3 4 5 6 7 8 9 10

Week

My June goals

_____

_____

_____

_____

_____

_____

In order to reach my goals, I will this week

_____

_____

_____

_____

_____

_____

This week will be great because

_____

_____

_____

_____

End of the week

Did I practice gratitude this week?

My personal successes this week

_____

_____

_____

_____

_____

_____

_____

Highlights of the week

_____

_____

_____

_____

_____

_____

_____

Week success	1	2	3	4	5	6	7	8	9	10
Felt alive this week	1	2	3	4	5	6	7	8	9	10
Daily routine success	1	2	3	4	5	6	7	8	9	10

Week

Beginning of the week
Did I reach previous week's goals?

My June goals

_____

_____

_____

_____

_____

_____

In order to reach my goals, I will this week

_____

_____

_____

_____

_____

_____

This week will be great because

_____

_____

_____

_____

End of the week

Did I have fun this week?

My personal successes this week

_____

_____

_____

_____

_____

_____

_____

Highlights of the week

_____

_____

_____

_____

_____

_____

Week success	1 2 3 4 5 6 7 8 9 10
Felt alive this week	1 2 3 4 5 6 7 8 9 10
Daily routine success	1 2 3 4 5 6 7 8 9 10

Week

My June goals

_____

_____

_____

_____

_____

In order to reach my goals, I will this week

_____

_____

_____

_____

_____

This week will be great because

_____

_____

_____

_____

End of the week

Did I contribute to others this week?

My personal successes this week

_____

_____

_____

_____

_____

_____

_____

Highlights of the week

_____

_____

_____

_____

_____

_____

_____

Week success	1 2 3 4 5 6 7 8 9 10
Felt alive this week	1 2 3 4 5 6 7 8 9 10
Daily routine success	1 2 3 4 5 6 7 8 9 10

June Highlights

Month Overall Success   1   2   3   4   5   6   7   8   9   10

JULY

Relationships	1	2	3	4	5	6	7	8	9	10
Health	1	2	3	4	5	6	7	8	9	10
Finances	1	2	3	4	5	6	7	8	9	10
Productivity	1	2	3	4	5	6	7	8	9	10
Creativity	1	2	3	4	5	6	7	8	9	10
Job/business	1	2	3	4	5	6	7	8	9	10
Self-esteem	1	2	3	4	5	6	7	8	9	10
Happiness	1	2	3	4	5	6	7	8	9	10

Last month review and loose ends

I want to experience these exciting, fun, joyful things in July

I want to read these books in July

_____

_____

_____

_____

_____

By July 31, I'm better at

_____

_____

_____

_____

My Daily Routine

Morning

Day

Evening

My 3-Month Goals

By September 30, 2019 I have

_____

_____

_____

_____

_____

_____

My July goals

By July 31, 2019 I have

_____

_____

_____

_____

_____

_____

Week

Beginning of the week

"All progress takes place outside the comfort zone"

— Michal John Bobak

In order to reach my goals, I will this week

_____

_____

_____

_____

_____

_____

_____

This week will be great because

_____

_____

_____

_____

End of the week

Did I have fun this week?

My personal successes this week

_____

_____

_____

_____

_____

_____

Highlights of the week

_____

_____

_____

_____

_____

_____

Week success	1 2 3 4 5 6 7 8 9 10

Week success   1 2 3 4 5 6 7 8 9 10
Felt alive this week 1 2 3 4 5 6 7 8 9 10
Daily routine success 1 2 3 4 5 6 7 8 9 10

Week

Beginning of the week
Did I reach previous week's goals?

My July goals

_____
_____
_____
_____
_____
_____

In order to reach my goals, I will this week

_____
_____
_____
_____
_____

This week will be great because

_____
_____
_____
_____

End of the week

Did I drink enough water this week?

My personal successes this week

_____

_____

_____

_____

_____

_____

_____

Highlights of the week

_____

_____

_____

_____

_____

_____

Week success	1	2	3	4	5	6	7	8	9	10
Felt alive this week	1	2	3	4	5	6	7	8	9	10
Daily routine success	1	2	3	4	5	6	7	8	9	10

Week

Beginning of the week
Did I reach previous week's goals?

My July goals

_____

_____

_____

_____

_____

_____

In order to reach my goals, I will this week

_____

_____

_____

_____

_____

_____

This week will be great because

_____

_____

_____

_____

End of the week
Did I express love this week ?

My personal successes this week

_____

_____

_____

_____

_____

_____

Highlights of the week

_____

_____

_____

_____

_____

_____

Week success	1 2 3 4 5 6 7 8 9 10
Felt alive this week	1 2 3 4 5 6 7 8 9 10
Daily routine success	1 2 3 4 5 6 7 8 9 10

Week

Beginning of the week
Did I reach previous week's goals?

My July goals

_____

_____

_____

_____

_____

_____

In order to reach my goals, I will this week

_____

_____

_____

_____

_____

_____

This week will be great because

_____

_____

_____

_____

End of the week

Did I have fun this week?

My personal successes this week

_____

_____

_____

_____

_____

_____

_____

Highlights of the week

_____

_____

_____

_____

_____

_____

_____

Week success	1	2	3	4	5	6	7	8	9	10
Felt alive this week	1	2	3	4	5	6	7	8	9	10
Daily routine success	1	2	3	4	5	6	7	8	9	10

Week

My July goals

In order to reach my goals, I will this week

This week will be great because

End of the week
Did I practice gratitude this week?

My personal successes this week

_____

_____

_____

_____

_____

_____

_____

Highlights of the week

_____

_____

_____

_____

_____

_____

Week success   1 2 3 4 5 6 7 8 9 10
Felt alive this week   1 2 3 4 5 6 7 8 9 10
Daily routine success   1 2 3 4 5 6 7 8 9 10

July Highlights

Month Overall Success   1   2   3   4   5   6   7   8   9   10

AUGUST

Relationships	1	2	3	4	5	6	7	8	9	10
Health	1	2	3	4	5	6	7	8	9	10
Finances	1	2	3	4	5	6	7	8	9	10
Productivity	1	2	3	4	5	6	7	8	9	10
Creativity	1	2	3	4	5	6	7	8	9	10
Job/business	1	2	3	4	5	6	7	8	9	10
Self-esteem	1	2	3	4	5	6	7	8	9	10
Happiness	1	2	3	4	5	6	7	8	9	10

Last month review and loose ends

I want to experience these exciting, fun, joyful things in August

I want to read these books in August

_____

_____

_____

_____

_____

By August 31, I'm better at

_____

_____

_____

_____

_____

My Daily Routine

Morning

Day

Evening

My 3-Month Goals

By September 30, 2019 I have

_____

_____

_____

_____

_____

My August Goals

By August 31, 2019 I have

_____

_____

_____

_____

_____

Week

Beginning of the week

"If you look closely, most overnight successes took a long time"

– Steve Jobs

In order to reach my goals, I will this week

_____

_____

_____

_____

_____

_____

_____

This week will be great because

_____

_____

_____

_____

End of the week
Did I have fun this week?

My personal successes this week

_____

_____

_____

_____

_____

_____

_____

Highlights of the week

_____

_____

_____

_____

_____

_____

_____

Week success	1	2	3	4	5	6	7	8	9	10
Felt alive this week	1	2	3	4	5	6	7	8	9	10
Daily routine success	1	2	3	4	5	6	7	8	9	10

Week

Beginning of the week
Did I reach previous week's goals?

My August goals

_____

_____

_____

_____

_____

_____

In order to reach my goals, I will this week

_____

_____

_____

_____

_____

This week will be great because

_____

_____

_____

_____

End of the week

Did I practice gratitude this week?

My personal successes this week

_____

_____

_____

_____

_____

_____

_____

Highlights of the week

_____

_____

_____

_____

_____

_____

_____

Week success	1	2	3	4	5	6	7	8	9	10
Felt alive this week	1	2	3	4	5	6	7	8	9	10
Daily routine success	1	2	3	4	5	6	7	8	9	10

Week

Beginning of the week
Did I reach previous week's goals?

My August goals

_____

_____

_____

_____

_____

In order to reach my goals, I will this week

_____

_____

_____

_____

_____

This week will be great because

_____

_____

_____

_____

End of the week

Did I drink enough water this week?

My personal successes this week

_____

_____

_____

_____

_____

_____

Highlights of the week

_____

_____

_____

_____

_____

_____

Week success	1 2 3 4 5 6 7 8 9 10
Felt alive this week	1 2 3 4 5 6 7 8 9 10
Daily routine success	1 2 3 4 5 6 7 8 9 10

Week

My August goals

In order to reach my goals, I will this week

This week will be great because

End of the week

Did I have fun this week?

My personal successes this week

_____

_____

_____

_____

_____

_____

_____

Highlights of the week

_____

_____

_____

_____

_____

_____

Week success	1 2 3 4 5 6 7 8 9 10
Felt alive this week	1 2 3 4 5 6 7 8 9 10
Daily routine success	1 2 3 4 5 6 7 8 9 10

Week

My August goals

_____

_____

_____

_____

_____

_____

In order to reach my goals, I will this week

_____

_____

_____

_____

_____

_____

This week will be great because

_____

_____

_____

_____

End of the week

Did I contribute to others this week?

My personal successes this week

_____

_____

_____

_____

_____

_____

Highlights of the week

_____

_____

_____

_____

_____

_____

Week success	1 2 3 4 5 6 7 8 9 10
Felt alive this week	1 2 3 4 5 6 7 8 9 10
Daily routine success	1 2 3 4 5 6 7 8 9 10

August Highlights

Month Overall Success   1   2   3   4   5   6   7   8   9   10

SEPTEMBER

Relationships	1	2	3	4	5	6	7	8	9	10
Health	1	2	3	4	5	6	7	8	9	10
Finances	1	2	3	4	5	6	7	8	9	10
Productivity	1	2	3	4	5	6	7	8	9	10
Creativity	1	2	3	4	5	6	7	8	9	10
Job/business	1	2	3	4	5	6	7	8	9	10
Self-esteem	1	2	3	4	5	6	7	8	9	10
Happiness	1	2	3	4	5	6	7	8	9	10

Last month review and loose ends

I want to experience these exciting, fun, joyful things in September

I want to read these books in September

By September 30, I'm better at

My Daily Routine

Morning

Day

Evening

My 3-Month Goals

By 30th September 2019 I have

My September goals

By 30th September 2019 I have (if different from above)

Week

"Don't let the fear of losing be greater than the excitement of winning"

— Robert Kiyosaki

In order to reach my goals, I will this week

_____

_____

_____

_____

_____

_____

This week will be great because

_____

_____

_____

_____

End of the week

Did I have fun this week?

My personal successes this week

_____

_____

_____

_____

_____

_____

_____

Highlights of the week

_____

_____

_____

_____

_____

_____

Week success   1 2 3 4 5 6 7 8 9 10
Felt alive this week 1 2 3 4 5 6 7 8 9 10
Daily routine success 1 2 3 4 5 6 7 8 9 10

Week

My September goals

_____

_____

_____

_____

_____

_____

In order to reach my goals, I will this week

_____

_____

_____

_____

_____

This week will be great because

_____

_____

_____

_____

End of the week

Did I practice gratitude this week ?

My personal successes this week

_____

_____

_____

_____

_____

_____

_____

Highlights of the week

_____

_____

_____

_____

_____

_____

_____

Week success	1	2	3	4	5	6	7	8	9	10
Felt alive this week	1	2	3	4	5	6	7	8	9	10
Daily routine success	1	2	3	4	5	6	7	8	9	10

Week

Beginning of the week
Did I reach previous week's goals?

My September goals

_____

_____

_____

_____

_____

_____

In order to reach my goals, I will this week

_____

_____

_____

_____

_____

_____

This week will be great because

_____

_____

_____

_____

End of the week

Did I enjoy life this week?

My personal successes this week

_____

_____

_____

_____

_____

_____

Highlights of the week

_____

_____

_____

_____

_____

_____

Week success	1 2 3 4 5 6 7 8 9 10
Felt alive this week	1 2 3 4 5 6 7 8 9 10
Daily routine success	1 2 3 4 5 6 7 8 9 10

Week

Beginning of the week
Did I reach previous week's goals?

My September goals

_____

_____

_____

_____

_____

_____

In order to reach my goals, I will this week

_____

_____

_____

_____

_____

_____

This week will be great because

_____

_____

_____

_____

End of the week

Did I drink enough water this week?

My personal successes this week

_____

_____

_____

_____

_____

_____

_____

Highlights of the week

_____

_____

_____

_____

_____

_____

_____

Week success	1 2 3 4 5 6 7 8 9 10
Felt alive this week	1 2 3 4 5 6 7 8 9 10
Daily routine success	1 2 3 4 5 6 7 8 9 10

Week

My September goals

_____

_____

_____

_____

_____

In order to reach my goals, I will this week

_____

_____

_____

_____

_____

This week will be great because

_____

_____

_____

_____

End of the week

Did I express love this week?

My personal successes this week

_____

_____

_____

_____

_____

_____

_____

Highlights of the week

_____

_____

_____

_____

_____

_____

Week success	1 2 3 4 5 6 7 8 9 10
Felt alive this week	1 2 3 4 5 6 7 8 9 10
Daily routine success	1 2 3 4 5 6 7 8 9 10

September Highlights

Month Overall Success   1   2   3   4   5   6   7   8   9   10

OCTOBER

Relationships	1 2 3 4 5 6 7 8 9 10
Health	1 2 3 4 5 6 7 8 9 10
Finances	1 2 3 4 5 6 7 8 9 10
Productivity	1 2 3 4 5 6 7 8 9 10
Creativity	1 2 3 4 5 6 7 8 9 10
Job/business	1 2 3 4 5 6 7 8 9 10
Self-esteem	1 2 3 4 5 6 7 8 9 10
Happiness	1 2 3 4 5 6 7 8 9 10

Last month review and loose ends

I want to experience these exciting, fun, joyful things in October

I want to read these books in October

By October 31, I'm better at

My Daily Routine

Morning

Day

Evening

My 3-Month Goals

By December 31, 2019 I have

My October Goals

By October 31, 2019 I have

Week

Beginning of the week

"The secret to success it to do the common thing uncommonly well"

– John D. Rockefeller Jr.

In order to reach my goals, I will this week

_____

_____

_____

_____

_____

_____

This week will be great because

_____

_____

_____

_____

End of the week
Did I have fun this week?

My personal successes this week

_____

_____

_____

_____

_____

_____

Highlights of the week

_____

_____

_____

_____

_____

_____

Week success	1	2	3	4	5	6	7	8	9	10
Felt alive this week	1	2	3	4	5	6	7	8	9	10
Daily routine success	1	2	3	4	5	6	7	8	9	10

Week

Beginning of the week
Did I reach previous week's goals?

My October goals

_____

_____

_____

_____

_____

_____

In order to reach my goals, I will this week

_____

_____

_____

_____

_____

_____

This week will be great because

_____

_____

_____

_____

End of the week
Did I express love this week?

My personal successes this week

_____

_____

_____

_____

_____

_____

_____

Highlights of the week

_____

_____

_____

_____

_____

_____

_____

Week success	1 2 3 4 5 6 7 8 9 10
Felt alive this week	1 2 3 4 5 6 7 8 9 10
Daily routine success	1 2 3 4 5 6 7 8 9 10

Week

Beginning of the week
Did I reach previous week's goals?

My October goals

_____

_____

_____

_____

_____

_____

In order to reach my goals, I will this week

_____

_____

_____

_____

_____

_____

This week will be great because

_____

_____

_____

_____

End of the week
Did I enjoy life this week?

My personal successes this week

_____

_____

_____

_____

_____

_____

Highlights of the week

_____

_____

_____

_____

_____

_____

Week success	1 2 3 4 5 6 7 8 9 10
Felt alive this week	1 2 3 4 5 6 7 8 9 10
Daily routine success	1 2 3 4 5 6 7 8 9 10

Week

Beginning of the week
Did I reach previous week's goals?

My October goals

_____

_____

_____

_____

_____

_____

In order to reach my goals, I will this week

_____

_____

_____

_____

_____

_____

This week will be great because

_____

_____

_____

_____

End of the week

Did I practice gratitude this week?

My personal successes this week

_____

_____

_____

_____

_____

_____

Highlights of the week

_____

_____

_____

_____

_____

_____

Week success	1 2 3 4 5 6 7 8 9 10
Felt alive this week	1 2 3 4 5 6 7 8 9 10
Daily routine success	1 2 3 4 5 6 7 8 9 10

Week

Beginning of the week
Did I reach previous week's goals?

My October goals

_____

_____

_____

_____

_____

In order to reach my goals, I will this week

_____

_____

_____

_____

_____

This week will be great because

_____

_____

_____

_____

End of the week

Did I drink enough water this week?

My personal successes this week

_____

_____

_____

_____

_____

_____

_____

Highlights of the week

_____

_____

_____

_____

_____

_____

_____

Week success	1	2	3	4	5	6	7	8	9	10
Felt alive this week	1	2	3	4	5	6	7	8	9	10
Daily routine success	1	2	3	4	5	6	7	8	9	10

October Highlights

Month Overall Success   1   2   3   4   5   6   7   8   9   10

NOVEMBER

Relationships	1	2	3	4	5	6	7	8	9	10
Health	1	2	3	4	5	6	7	8	9	10
Finances	1	2	3	4	5	6	7	8	9	10
Productivity	1	2	3	4	5	6	7	8	9	10
Creativity	1	2	3	4	5	6	7	8	9	10
Job/business	1	2	3	4	5	6	7	8	9	10
Self-esteem	1	2	3	4	5	6	7	8	9	10
Happiness	1	2	3	4	5	6	7	8	9	10

Last month review and loose ends

I want to experience these exciting, fun, joyful things in November

I want to read these books in November

_____

_____

_____

_____

_____

By November 30, I'm better at

_____

_____

_____

_____

My Daily Routine

Morning

Day

Evening

My 3-Month Goals

By December 31, 2019 I have

_____

_____

_____

_____

_____

_____

My November Goals

By November 30, 2019 I have

_____

_____

_____

_____

_____

_____

Week

_____

"I never dreamed about success, I worked for it"

– Estee Lauder

_____

In order to reach my goals, I will this week

....

....

....

....

....

....

This week will be great because

....

....

....

....

End of the week
Did I have fun this week?

My personal successes this week

_____

_____

_____

_____

_____

_____

_____

Highlights of the week

_____

_____

_____

_____

_____

_____

_____

Week success	1 2 3 4 5 6 7 8 9 10
Felt alive this week	1 2 3 4 5 6 7 8 9 10
Daily routine success	1 2 3 4 5 6 7 8 9 10

Week

Beginning of the week
Did I reach previous week's goals?

My November goals

In order to reach my goals, I will this week

This week will be great because

End of the week

Did I express love this week ?

My personal successes this week

_____

_____

_____

_____

_____

_____

_____

Highlights of the week

_____

_____

_____

_____

_____

_____

Week success	1 2 3 4 5 6 7 8 9 10
Felt alive this week	1 2 3 4 5 6 7 8 9 10
Daily routine success	1 2 3 4 5 6 7 8 9 10

Week

Beginning of the week
Did I reach previous week's goals?

My November goals

In order to reach my goals, I will this week

This week will be great because

End of the week

Did I drink enough water this week?

My personal successes this week

_____

_____

_____

_____

_____

_____

_____

Highlights of the week

_____

_____

_____

_____

_____

_____

_____

Week success	1 2 3 4 5 6 7 8 9 10
Felt alive this week	1 2 3 4 5 6 7 8 9 10
Daily routine success	1 2 3 4 5 6 7 8 9 10

Week

My November goals

_____

_____

_____

_____

_____

_____

In order to reach my goals, I will this week

_____

_____

_____

_____

_____

_____

This week will be great because

_____

_____

_____

_____

End of the week

Did I practice gratitude this week?

My personal successes this week

_____

_____

_____

_____

_____

_____

Highlights of the week

_____

_____

_____

_____

_____

_____

Week success	1 2 3 4 5 6 7 8 9 10
Felt alive this week	1 2 3 4 5 6 7 8 9 10
Daily routine success	1 2 3 4 5 6 7 8 9 10

Week

Beginning of the week
Did I reach previous week's goals?

My November goals

_____

_____

_____

_____

_____

_____

In order to reach my goals, I will this week

_____

_____

_____

_____

_____

This week will be great because

_____

_____

_____

_____

End of the week

Did I contribute to others this week ?

My personal successes this week

_____

_____

_____

_____

_____

_____

Highlights of the week

_____

_____

_____

_____

_____

_____

Week success	1 2 3 4 5 6 7 8 9 10
Felt alive this week	1 2 3 4 5 6 7 8 9 10
Daily routine success	1 2 3 4 5 6 7 8 9 10

November Highlights

Month Overall Success   1   2   3   4   5   6   7   8   9   10

DECEMBER

Relationships	1	2	3	4	5	6	7	8	9	10
Health	1	2	3	4	5	6	7	8	9	10
Finances	1	2	3	4	5	6	7	8	9	10
Productivity	1	2	3	4	5	6	7	8	9	10
Creativity	1	2	3	4	5	6	7	8	9	10
Job/business	1	2	3	4	5	6	7	8	9	10
Self-esteem	1	2	3	4	5	6	7	8	9	10
Happiness	1	2	3	4	5	6	7	8	9	10

Last month review and loose ends

I want to experience these exciting, fun, joyful things in May

I want to read these books in December

_____

_____

_____

_____

_____

By December 31, I'm better at

_____

_____

_____

_____

My Daily Routine

Morning

Day

Evening

My 3-Months Goals

By December 31, 2019 I have

_____

_____

_____

_____

_____

_____

My December Goals

By December 31, 2019 I have (if different from above)

_____

_____

_____

_____

_____

_____

Week

"Success is not final, failure is not fatal: it is the courage to continue that counts"

— Winston Churchill

In order to reach my goals, I will this week

_____

_____

_____

_____

_____

_____

This week will be great because

_____

_____

_____

_____

End of the week
Did I have fun this week?

My personal successes this week

_____

_____

_____

_____

_____

_____

_____

Highlights of the week

_____

_____

_____

_____

_____

_____

_____

Week success	1 2 3 4 5 6 7 8 9 10
Felt alive this week	1 2 3 4 5 6 7 8 9 10
Daily routine success	1 2 3 4 5 6 7 8 9 10

Week

Beginning of the week
Did I reach previous week's goals?

My December goals

_____

_____

_____

_____

_____

_____

In order to reach my goals, I will this week

_____

_____

_____

_____

_____

This week will be great because

_____

_____

_____

_____

End of the week
Did I have fun this week?

My personal successes this week

_____

_____

_____

_____

_____

_____

_____

Highlights of the week

_____

_____

_____

_____

_____

_____

_____

Week success	1 2 3 4 5 6 7 8 9 10
Felt alive this week	1 2 3 4 5 6 7 8 9 10
Daily routine success	1 2 3 4 5 6 7 8 9 10

Week

My December goals

_____

_____

_____

_____

_____

_____

In order to reach my goals, I will this week

_____

_____

_____

_____

_____

_____

This week will be great because

_____

_____

_____

_____

End of the week

Did I enjoy life this week?

My personal successes this week

_____

_____

_____

_____

_____

_____

_____

Highlights of the week

_____

_____

_____

_____

_____

_____

_____

Week success	1	2	3	4	5	6	7	8	9	10
Felt alive this week	1	2	3	4	5	6	7	8	9	10
Daily routine success	1	2	3	4	5	6	7	8	9	10

Week

My December goals

_____

_____

_____

_____

_____

_____

In order to reach my goals, I will this week

_____

_____

_____

_____

_____

_____

This week will be great because

_____

_____

_____

_____

End of the week
Did I drink enough water this week?

My personal successes this week

_____

_____

_____

_____

_____

_____

Highlights of the week

_____

_____

_____

_____

_____

_____

Week success | 1 | 2 | 3 | 4 | 5 | 6 | 7 | 8 | 9 | 10
Felt alive this week | 1 | 2 | 3 | 4 | 5 | 6 | 7 | 8 | 9 | 10
Daily routine success | 1 | 2 | 3 | 4 | 5 | 6 | 7 | 8 | 9 | 10

Week

Beginning of the week
Did I reach previous week's goals?

My December goals

_____

_____

_____

_____

_____

_____

In order to reach my goals, I will this week

_____

_____

_____

_____

_____

_____

This week will be great because

_____

_____

_____

_____

End of the week

Did I express love this week?

My personal successes this week

_____

_____

_____

_____

_____

_____

_____

Highlights of the week

_____

_____

_____

_____

_____

_____

Week success	1	2	3	4	5	6	7	8	9	10
Felt alive this week	1	2	3	4	5	6	7	8	9	10
Daily routine success	1	2	3	4	5	6	7	8	9	10

December Highlights

Month Overall Success   1   2   3   4   5   6   7   8   9   10

Looking over the past 12 months

Did I reach my goals? If not all, did I reach some of them?
Why/why not?

Did I see any progress in the weekly and monthly ratings?
Why/why not?

Was I more productive than previous years?
Why/why not?

Was I more successful than previous years?
Why/why not?

Am I satisfied with the year as a whole?
Why/why not?

28724804R00136

Made in the USA
Lexington, KY
19 January 2019